CONTENTS

VISIBLE ENERGY

We are bathed in light. From a distance of 150 million kilometres the Sun sends light streaming down on us. Our eyes have evolved to make use of this light. Light also helps to keep us warm.

Light is a form of energy that travels very quickly. Burning sticks, hot coals and light bulbs all give off light. The Sun gives us most of the light that we use.

Seeing is the main way humans use light. The eye collects light heading

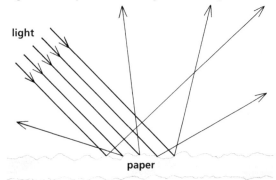

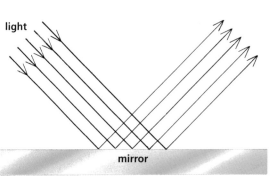

▲ Light travels in straight lines. You can see that beams of light are straight when dust or mist in the air reflects some of the light, as in this forest scene.

towards it. Special cells inside the eye sense the light and send signals to the brain. Somehow the brain turns these signals into pictures.

Dull, shiny or see-through?

When light hits an object, some of the energy is taken in (absorbed). The rest either bounces back (reflects) or travels straight through the object. Glass and water are transparent (see-through) as they let light travel straight through them without absorbing much energy. Objects that you cannot see through reflect and absorb light.

Shiny objects with a smooth surface reflect light very well. Dark, rough objects do not reflect very well, so they absorb most of the light hitting them. The energy absorbed from light warms the object up. This is partly why we get hot on a sunny day in summer.

▲ Most smooth surfaces, such as paper, are actually quite uneven, and reflect light in all directions. Very smooth and shiny surfaces, such as mirrors, reflect light in a more orderly way.

▶ Very still water is smooth enough to act as an excellent mirror. These mountains in South America are reflected in the still lake.

WAVE BASICS

The British physicist Thomas Young (1773–1829) proved that light consists of waves.

Wave motion consists of a series of peaks and troughs (a). Every wave has a wavelength: the distance the wave travels between two peaks (one complete cycle). The height of each peak or trough is the amplitude of a wave.

The frequency of a wave is the number of cycles the wave goes through every second. The bottom wave (b) is twice the frequency of the top one. Higher frequency waves have shorter wavelengths.

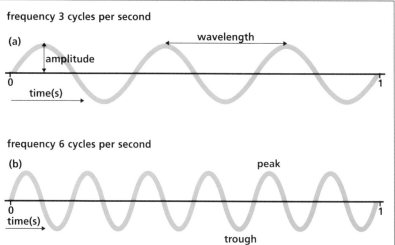

frequency 3 cycles per second

(a) amplitude wavelength

0 time(s) 1

frequency 6 cycles per second

(b) peak

0 time(s) 1

trough

Light waves

Light travels as a series of tiny waves. When a lamp makes light, the energy streams out like ripples crossing a pond. The distance between two peaks in a series of ripples is called the wavelength. Light waves also have a wavelength. The wavelength of light is very small – you could fit 2500 of the smallest light waves in just one millimetre.

Colours

When we see white light, we are actually looking at many colours mixed together.

▲ In this puppet theatre from Indonesia, the puppets are held between the light source and a semi-transparent screen. The puppets block the light, making dark shadows on the bright screen.

These colours can be split up so we can see them. A rainbow is made when drops of water separate the colours in sunlight. The same thing can be done using a prism (a triangular piece of glass). The pattern of colours is called a spectrum.

Most objects are coloured because of the way they reflect light. White objects reflect all the colours. Black objects hardly reflect any light at all. Coloured objects reflect back some of the colours, but absorb others.

Each colour is light of a different wavelength. Red light has the longest wavelength, while violet light has the shortest. Waves with a longer wavelength than red light are invisible: they are called infrared (IR) waves. At the other end of the spectrum, invisible ultraviolet (UV) waves have wavelengths shorter than violet light.

Bending light

If you hold a straight stick so that it has one end under water, you will see that the stick does not look straight. Light coming from the end of the stick is bent as it comes out of the water.

If you stand on top of a cliff above a beach and watch the waves angling in, you may notice that they sometimes bend as they reach the shore. Waves slow down as the water gets shallower, and because the waves are coming in at an angle, one end is slowed down first. This makes the waves bend.

Light can be bent in the same way: this is called refraction. Light travels more slowly in glass than in air, so when light rays hit a piece of glass at an angle, they bend. The lenses and prisms we use in spectacles, cameras and binoculars all bend light in this way.

Light travels 9461 million million kilometres in a year. Astronomers call this distance a light year. They use it to measure the distances to stars and galaxies.

key words
- absorb
- light year
- reflection
- refraction
- transparent
- wavelength

▶ If you put one end of a straight stick in water, it appears to bend where it enters the water (a). This is because light rays from the underwater end of the stick bend as they move from water into air (b). This fools the eye into seeing the end of the stick nearer to the surface than it actually is.

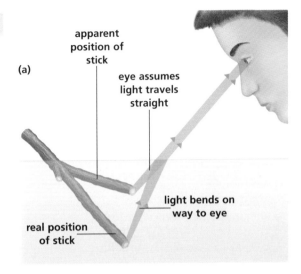

(a)

apparent position of stick

eye assumes light travels straight

light bends on way to eye

real position of stick

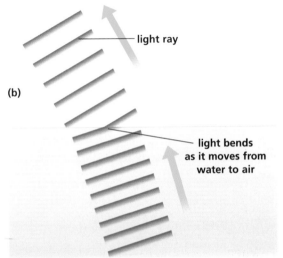

(b)

light ray

light bends as it moves from water to air

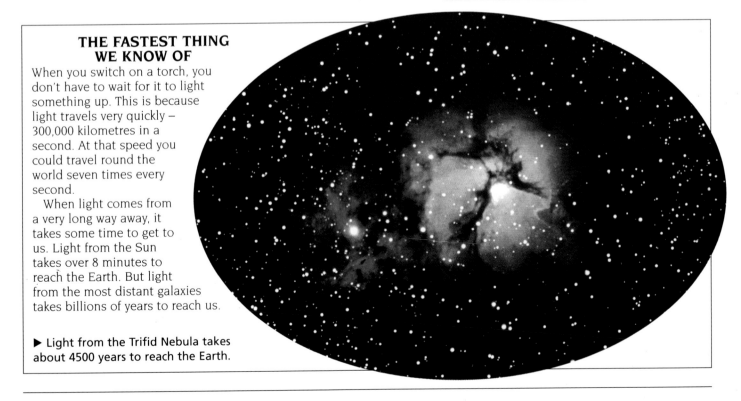

THE FASTEST THING WE KNOW OF

When you switch on a torch, you don't have to wait for it to light something up. This is because light travels very quickly – 300,000 kilometres in a second. At that speed you could travel round the world seven times every second.

When light comes from a very long way away, it takes some time to get to us. Light from the Sun takes over 8 minutes to reach the Earth. But light from the most distant galaxies takes billions of years to reach us.

▶ Light from the Trifid Nebula takes about 4500 years to reach the Earth.

THE COLOURS OF THE RAINBOW

The storm is over. After the crashing violence of the thunder and lightning, the graceful arc of a rainbow extends across the sky. The band of colours a rainbow produces is called a spectrum.

When we see white light, we are actually looking at lots of different colours mixed together. White light can be split up so that the separate colours can be seen. A triangular piece of glass (a prism) is very good at doing this as it bends (refracts) light. The different colours bend by different amounts, so they spread out and form a rainbow pattern. Each colour is a different wavelength of light.

Rainbows

Rainbows are made when there are lots of raindrops in the air. The drops reflect light that is coming from behind you. This is why you never see the Sun in the same direction as a rainbow.

When the light enters a raindrop, it splits into colours. The different colours reflect off the back of the raindrop and split up even further as they come out again. Only one colour from each raindrop will reach your eye. However, you see the whole rainbow, because there are millions of drops reflecting light towards you.

▶ A Brocken spectre is a ghostly figure surrounded by a rainbow, sometimes seen by mountaineers. The 'spectre' is actually the viewer's shadow falling on mist or cloud. The halo around it is produced when sunlight is split into tiny rainbows by water drops in the mist or cloud.

white light

prism

🔵 key words

- prism
- rainbow
- reflection
- spectrum

◀ The tiny spectra in this picture are made by stars. The light from the stars was split up by a prism inserted into the telescope used to take the picture. The spectrum for each star is different in detail, as each star produces slightly different light.

▼ A prism is a triangular-shaped piece of glass that can be used to split white light into a spectrum. White light is partly split as it enters the prism. The colours then travel across the prism in straight lines to be spread even further apart as they leave the glass on the other side.

spectrum

If you are looking down on a rainbow from high up (from a mountain, for example), you can sometimes see it as a complete circle, not just an arc.

Extending the spectrum

Sunlight contains other waves besides the ones in the visible spectrum. Just beyond the red end of the spectrum is infrared (IR) radiation, with wavelengths longer than red light. We cannot see IR, but it is given off by warm objects. The remote control on a TV uses infrared.

At the other end of the spectrum is ultraviolet (UV) radiation, which has wavelengths shorter than violet light. UV from the Sun gives us a suntan.

IT'S A COLOURFUL WORLD

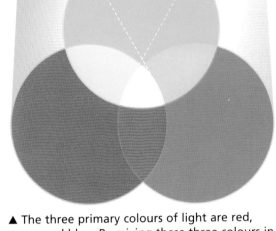

Caught in the light, a soap bubble shimmers with a beautiful and complex pattern of colours. This is an example of the gift evolution has given us – a marvellous colour-sensitive eye.

All colours come from light. White light is really a mixture of different colours. There are several ways to separate these colours so that we can see them. The surface of a bubble does this, and so do drops of rainwater, which hang in the air and make a rainbow.

▼ If a disc is painted with the three primary colours and then spun very fast, we see the disc as white.

▲ The three primary colours of light are red, green and blue. By mixing these three colours in different combinations, it is possible to make any other colour.

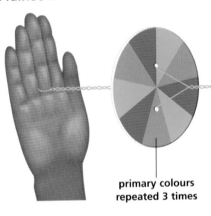

primary colours
repeated 3 times

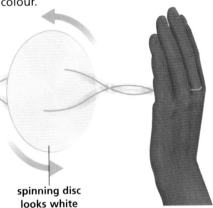

spinning disc
looks white

The colours of light

The pattern of colours in a rainbow is the same as that made by a prism (red to violet) and is called a spectrum. Light travels in the form of waves. The different colours of the spectrum have different wavelengths. If you think of light as being like ripples on the surface of a pond, the wavelength is the distance between the wave peaks. The wavelength of visible light is very small: between 1350 and 2500 light waves would fit in a millimetre, depending on the colour of the light.

Some objects, such as lamps, produce their own light. If they are producing all of the colours, they look white. If they only

◀ A rainbow over Victoria Falls in Zimbabwe. Rainbows are made when sunlight is split into a spectrum of colours by tiny water droplets in the air.

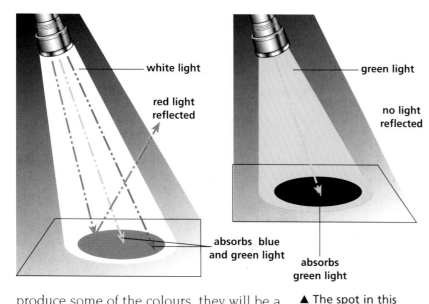

white light

red light
reflected

absorbs blue
and green light

green light

no light
reflected

absorbs
green light

produce some of the colours, they will be a colour of the spectrum. Yellow street lamps are yellow simply because they are only making yellow light.

The colours of things

Most of the objects we see reflect light to our eyes. An object that reflects all of the colours equally well (such as a snowman) will look white. A tarmac road looks black because it is hardly reflecting any light at all. Other colours are produced if the object is reflecting some of the light hitting it and absorbing the rest. For example, a red car reflects red light, and absorbs the other colours of the spectrum.

▲ The spot in this picture absorbs blue and green light, but reflects red. In white light the spot looks red, but in green light, no light is reflected, and it looks black.

🔵 key words

- absorb
- colour
- primary colour
- prism
- rainbow
- reflect
- spectrum
- wavelength

◄ The primary colours of pigments (paints, dyes and inks) are red, blue and yellow. You can mix them to make all other colours except white. Mixing all these pigment colours makes black.

COLOUR VISION

Surprisingly, the eye contains only three types of colour-sensitive cell. These cells (called cones) are at the back of the eye (the retina). The cones respond to red, green and blue light. The brain makes out all the other colours by combining the signals from these cells. Yellow light stimulates the red and green cells, but not the blue cells. The brain has learnt to recognize this combined signal as being due to yellow light.

Some of the colours that we see are not part of the spectrum at all. For example, there is no wavelength of light for the colour brown. Such colours are invented by the brain using some combination of signals from the eye.

We can use the way the brain recognizes colours to fool it into seeing colours that are not really there. A colour TV picture is made up of tiny red, green and blue dots close together. We see a whole variety of colours because these dots are made to shine at different brightnesses. A yellow shirt is shown on the screen by making the red and green dots shine much more brightly than the blue ones. This produces exactly the same signal to the brain as yellow light. In this way the eye is 'tricked' into seeing a yellow shirt.

▼ You can see any colour on your TV screen, but if you look at the screen closely enough, you will see that the picture is made up of tiny dots of just three colours: red, green and blue.

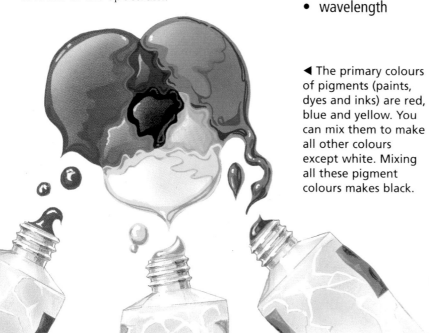

BOUNCING AND BENDING LIGHT

You are the captain of a ship on a foggy night. You know there are rocks about, so you are glad to see the bright light from a lighthouse. Lighthouses don't just use a big light bulb. There is also a curved mirror to reflect the light forwards and a curved lens to bend it into a powerful beam.

Mirrors reflect light well because they are smooth and shiny. The earliest mirrors were probably polished metal, but now we use coated glass.

Flat mirrors have a shiny aluminium coating on the back of a piece of glass. When you look in a flat mirror, your image seems to be behind the mirror. It is also the wrong way round. Ambulances have words written backwards on them so they can be read the right way round in a car's mirror.

Curved mirrors

Behind the bulb in a torch there is a shiny curved surface. It reflects light from the bulb forwards in a beam. Shapes that curve inwards like this are called concave. This is the sort of mirror used in lighthouses. Concave mirrors are also used in some

▶ Polishing the main mirror for the Hubble Space Telescope. This huge mirror is used to gather light from distant galaxies. To get a sharp image the mirror has to be very, very smooth. The engineers making it wear masks and special suits to keep off every speck of dust.

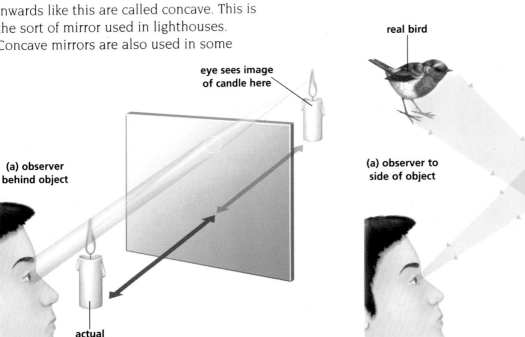

eye sees image of candle here

(a) observer behind object

actual candle

real bird

(a) observer to side of object

image of bird

◀ The image in a mirror seems to be behind the mirror. The eye cannot tell the difference between the light reflected off the mirror and that coming from a real object the same distance away as the image.

telescopes, because they are very good at collecting light.

Convex mirrors curve outwards. They let you see a very wide picture. You sometimes see them placed at difficult road junctions so drivers can see what is coming round the corner.

Lenses

If you look at a flower under a magnifying glass, it seems much bigger. The same lens can also be used to make a picture. If you were to hold it up in front of a window, you could make a picture of the window on a piece of paper. The picture would be smaller than the window and upside-down. A camera uses a lens in just this way to make a picture on a film. The picture does not have to be smaller. A projector uses a lens to throw a very large picture on a screen. Cameras, magnifying glasses and projectors all use lenses that are fat in the middle and thin at the edges. This shape is called convex. Convex lenses bend light so

multiple convex and concave lenses

▶ A camera 'lens' is actually made up of many different lenses. These help to make the image sharp and stop objects from having a halo of colours around the edges.

that it comes together. They are also sometimes called converging lenses.

Some lenses are shaped so they are thin in the middle and fat at the edges. These are concave lenses, and they make light spread out. Such lenses are also known as diverging lenses. Concave lenses are used in spectacles for short-sighted people, who cannot see things that are a long way away.

Special lenses

The lens in our eye is the one we use most often. It has the wonderful ability to get fatter and thinner. Without this, we would have trouble focusing on objects.

A single lens makes pictures that are slightly blurry. Sometimes the colours are not quite right either. To get round this problem, camera and projector 'lenses' are actually made up of several lenses.

key words

- concave
- converging lens
- convex
- diverging lens
- magnifying glass

light

convex lens

focal point

light

concave lens

▲ A convex (converging) lens bends light so that it narrows to a point. A concave (diverging) lens spreads light out.

WINDOWS ON THE WORLD

We get 80 per cent of our information about the world around us through a small pair of sense organs – our eyes. For animals such as birds of prey, sight is even more important. Nearly all animals have eyes of some sort. Even plants and very simple creatures have ways of sensing light.

The eyes are our organs of sight, just as our ears are our organs of hearing. The eye is a means of turning light into electrical signals. The brain takes these signals and uses them to make the colourful, moving world we see about us.

The parts of the eye

At the front of the eye is a clear, curved cornea, which bends light as it passes into the eyeball. It is covered by a thin membrane called the conjunctiva. A lens inside the eye bends the light further. Together the lens and cornea focus light onto a sheet of light-sensitive cells at the back of the eye called the retina. When these cells are stimulated by light, they send electrical signals to the brain. The image that the eye makes on the retina is actually upside down, but our brain turns the image the right way up.

▶ The parts of the human eye.

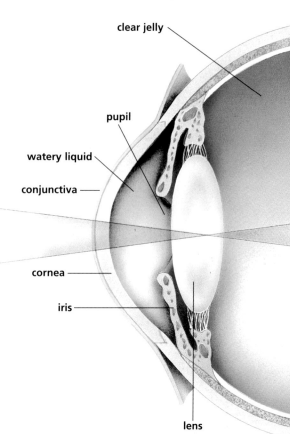

clear jelly

pupil

watery liquid

conjunctiva

cornea

iris

lens

🔵 key words
- compound eye
- cone
- iris
- lens
- pupil
- retina
- rod

Behind the cornea is a sheet of muscle (the iris) with a small round hole in the centre (the pupil). When the light is very bright, the brain sends a signal to the iris to contract, making the pupil smaller. This cuts down the amount of light entering the eye. Without this, we would be dazzled on a bright sunny day. If it is dark, then the iris relaxes, opening the pupil to let in as much light as possible.

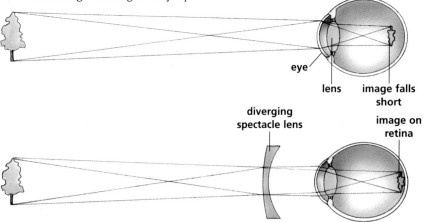

eye

lens   image falls short

diverging spectacle lens

image on retina

▲ In short sight, the eye's own lens cannot focus the image on the retina at back of the eye (top). This is corrected by wearing diverging (concave) lenses.

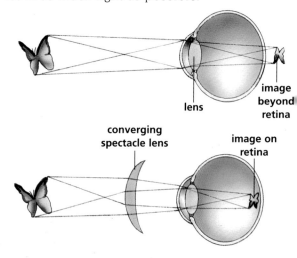

image beyond retina

lens

converging spectacle lens

image on retina

▲ In long sight, the eye's own lens focuses the image beyond the retina (top). This is corrected by wearing converging (convex) lenses.

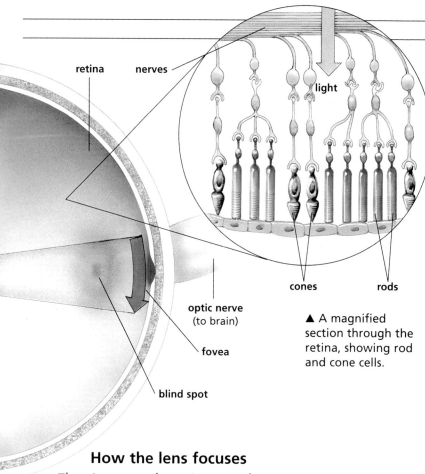

retina nerves

light

optic nerve
(to brain)

fovea

blind spot

cones rods

▲ A magnified
section through the
retina, showing rod
and cone cells.

How the lens focuses

The picture on the retina must be sharp if we are going to see clearly. Light is partly focused by the curved cornea, but it cannot focus objects that are close and distant things at the same time. To cope with this problem, the eye has a lens that can change shape. Muscles attached to the lens (the ciliary muscles) can contract to make the lens thin, for looking at distant objects. When the ciliary muscles relax, the lens becomes more curved, for close focus.

The retina

The retina contains cone-shaped cells that can detect colours. There are also rod-shaped cells that can see in dim light. Rods are not sensitive to colour. This is why things look rather grey at night.

In the centre of the retina is a small yellow area (the fovea) where each cell has its own connection to the brain. In other parts of the retina, many cells have to share a connection. The fovea lets us see in detail, but this only happens at the centre of the image. (Notice that you can make out only a few words on this page at a time). To make up for this, the brain continually moves the eyes back and forth to scan the whole image.

Other eyes

The structure of an animal's eye is often a good clue to how it lives. Owls, cats and other creatures that are mostly active at night have very large pupils so that they can gather in as much light as possible. Dolphins have 7000 times more rods in their eyes than humans do, which helps them to see in the dim light underwater.

▶ You can prove that your eyes have a blind spot using this picture. Cover your right eye, and focus on the blue dot with your left one. Keep concentrating on the blue dot, and move the page towards you until the red cross disappears. It has vanished because the image of it is focused on your blind spot.

+   ●

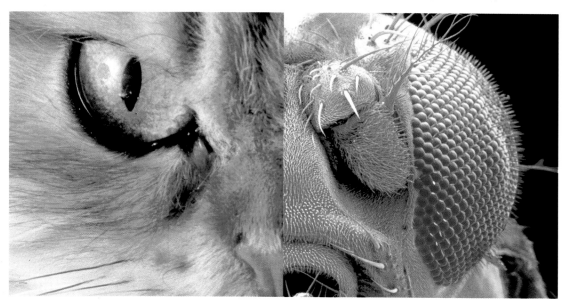

◀ A cat's eye and a fly's compound eye. A cat's pupil is a slit because it is a night hunter. At night, a slit can open much wider than a round pupil, so the cat's eye can take in as much light as possible. A fly's compound eye has 4000 individual tubes, with a lens at one end and light-sensitive cells at the other. The fly's brain puts together the tiny images from each tube to get an image of the world.

CATCHING LIGHT

Cameras are not just used for taking holiday snaps. They can reveal a world that we would not normally see. High-speed cameras can freeze very fast motion so we can see what is happening. They can even photograph a bullet in flight!

Cameras use a lens (a specially curved piece of glass) to make a small, upside-down picture on a film. The film is made from special chemicals that react to light. The film 'remembers' the picture as a pattern of chemicals that have been changed by the light. The film can then be developed using other chemicals to make the picture visible.

When you take a photograph, a metal blind called the shutter slides to one side. This lets light fall on the film. The shutter closes again after a short time. To get to the film, the light has to pass through an adjustable hole called the iris. If you are taking a photograph in dim light, the iris needs to be wide open to let as much light as possible fall on the film.

The right exposure

A picture will only come out correctly if the right amount of light is used. This can be done either by using a lot of light (big iris opening) for a very short time, or not much

▶ A high-speed camera was used to take this photo of a bullet frozen in flight as it cuts through a playing card.

▼ Just the right amount of light needs to fall on a film to get a good photograph. Too little light will make the photo very dark and murky (left). Too much light will make the photograph too bright and wash out the colours (right).

light (small iris opening) for longer. The combination of light and time is called the exposure.

Simple cameras used to have two or three exposure settings. These were labelled as bright, slightly cloudy or overcast. Most cameras today have light-sensitive circuits that set the exposure automatically.

Stay sharp

The picture formed by the lens will only be sharp if the lens is the right distance from the film. When the object you are taking a picture of is close, the lens needs to be moved away from the film. When the object is distant, the lens needs to be moved

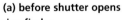
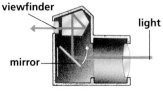

key words

- exposure
- film
- focusing
- iris
- lens
- shutter

▼ Press photographers at the Wimbledon tennis tournament. Professional photographers today use very sophisticated camera equipment.

Special types of camera

High-speed cameras use very sensitive films that can capture an image in a tiny instant. The shutter can also open and close very quickly. This helps to freeze the picture of a rapidly moving object (such as a bullet).

The lens in a digital camera makes its picture on a light-sensitive electronic plate called a charge-coupled device (CCD). Instead of recording the picture onto film, the CCD records information about colour and light levels as a pattern of electric charge. The information is then digitized and stored on something similar to a computer disk. You can look at the picture you have just taken on a screen, so that you can decide if you want to keep it or not.

Movie cameras work rather like ordinary cameras, except that they take lots of separate pictures (usually 24) every second. Each picture holds a frozen image of motion. When the pictures on the developed film are projected onto a screen at the right speed, the eye is fooled into seeing people and things moving about.

closer to the film. Changing the position of the lens like this is called focusing. Many cameras today can focus themselves. A tiny computer in the camera looks at how fuzzy the picture is. The computer controls a motor that moves the lens back and forth until the picture is sharp.

THE SLR CAMERA

Single-lens reflex (SLR) cameras are often used by professionals and other keen photographers.

There is a mirror behind the lens that reflects light to the viewfinder. The photographer can then see exactly what is coming through the lens. An electronic circuit measures the light coming through the lens to set the exposure.

The mirror prevents the light from reaching the shutter, so just before the picture is taken it flips up out of the way, so that light falls on the film when the shutter opens.

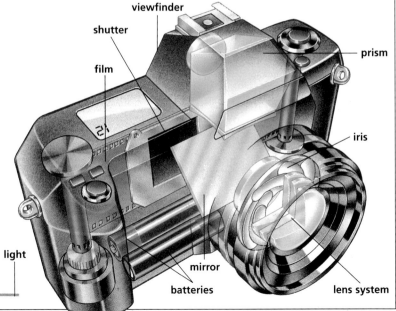

(a) before shutter opens
viewfinder
light
(b) as shutter opens
mirror
light
film

viewfinder
shutter
film
prism
iris
mirror
batteries
lens system

PAINTING WITH LIGHT

In the camera, photographic film is exposed to light from the object.

object being photographed

(a)

light from object

lens focuses light on film

We all enjoy our holiday photographs, or those embarrassing ones from the party we went to, but photography has some serious uses as well. There have been haunting images of starvation in Africa as well as pictures taken on the Moon. We have even photographed the moment when a human life begins.

Photographs are made in three steps. First light is allowed to fall on a film. Next the film is turned into a negative (a picture in which the dark parts of an object look light, and the light bits look dark). Finally a print is made from the negative. The print is the photograph that we look at.

Taking a photograph

A black-and-white film is made from thin plastic coated with a light-sensitive chemical containing silver.

To take a picture, light is let into the camera by opening a shutter. This is called exposing the film. Where a lot of light hits the film, the light changes the chemical on those parts of the film. On other parts of the film not as much light falls, so there is less change in the chemical.

Making a negative

The process of turning an exposed film into a negative is called development. There are three stages.

First of all, the film is dipped in a liquid called the developer. The developer reacts with the exposed chemicals in the film, making them release tiny pieces of silver.

▶ When you press the shutter button on a camera, the shutter opens and light falls briefly on the film (a). There is now an image of the scene on the film, but it can't be seen (b). Developing the film (c) produces a negative version of the scene on the film (d). The negative is put in an enlarger (e), and printed onto photographic paper. Now the light and dark areas on the photo correspond to the light and dark areas in the original scene (f).

(c)

developing tank

exposed film

(b)

The film is developed to make a negative image.

film

negative

(d)

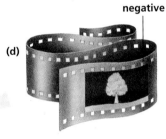

An enlarger is used to make the image bigger. It shines light through the negative onto paper. This can be done in dim red light – bright white light would turn the light-sensitive paper white, and the image would be lost.

(f)

enlarger

(e)

red light

light-sensitive paper

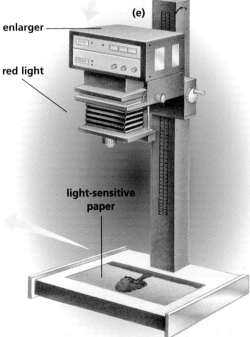

positive image

Where lots of the film chemical has been exposed, there will be many spots of silver.

Next the film is dipped in another chemical called fixer. The fixer reacts with the chemicals on the film, making them easy to wash off. It also sticks the pieces of silver firmly on the film. Finally the film is washed in water to rinse away all the unused chemicals.

The film is now transparent in some places, and dark in others where the silver has built up. The dark places are where the most light fell when the film was exposed, so the result is a negative image (black where the scene was bright, light where the scene was dark).

Printing

Pictures are printed on special paper with a light-sensitive coating. To do this, you shine light through the negative onto the paper. Where the negative is black, not much light gets through and the paper is not exposed. The transparent parts of the negative let a lot of light onto the paper, exposing the light-sensitive coating.

The paper is then developed by a three-stage process, just like the negative was. At the end of this, the paper has black areas (where silver has built up) and white parts (no silver and the paper shows through) in the right places. It is now a positive image.

▲ A photograph taken in about 1843 by the Englishman William Fox Talbot (1800–1877). The first ever photograph was taken in 1826 by the Frenchman Nicéphore Niepce, but it was Talbot who invented the modern method of making a negative from which many prints can be made.

COLOUR PHOTOGRAPHY

Developing and printing colour photographs is a bit like doing black-and-white ones – three times over.

The colour film has three layers: one is sensitive to red, one to green and one to blue. These are the three primary colours of light – our eyes and brains can be given the sensation of any colour just by mixing red,

green and blue light in different amounts.

The negative made from the exposed colour film is called a colour-reversed negative. Colour prints are made by passing first red, then green, then blue light through the negative onto special paper that also has three sensitive layers. The print ends up with the right combination of colours.

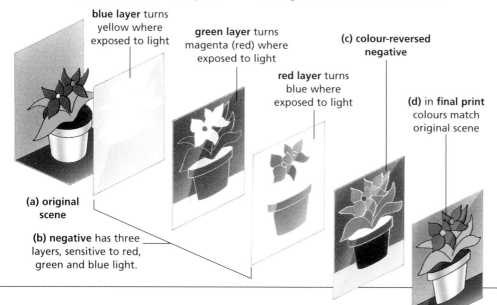

blue layer turns yellow where exposed to light

green layer turns magenta (red) where exposed to light

red layer turns blue where exposed to light

(c) colour-reversed negative

(d) in final print colours match original scene

(a) original scene

(b) negative has three layers, sensitive to red, green and blue light.

● **key words**
- camera
- development
- exposure
- film
- negative
- primary colours
- print
- shutter

MOVING PICTURES

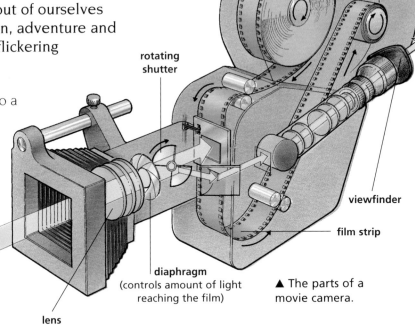

A good film takes us out of ourselves into a world of action, adventure and romance – simply using flickering pictures on a screen.

A movie is a series of still images projected onto a screen very quickly. You see it as a smoothly changing picture because the images are timed to trick your eye. Your eye will continue to see an image for about a twentieth of a second after it has disappeared (this is called persistence of vision). So the eye is still 'holding' the last image when the next one appears.

sprocket holes
(to hold film and move it on)

rotating shutter

viewfinder

film strip

diaphragm
(controls amount of light reaching the film)

▲ The parts of a movie camera.

lens

Filming a movie

Movie cameras capture the light coming from moving objects and use it to freeze an image – quickly, so the images are not blurred by the object's movement. The lens captures the light and directs it onto a film. (Movie film is light-sensitive, like ordinary

▼ These photographs of a cat falling were taken by photography pioneer Etienne-Jules Marey in the 1890s. He wanted to try to capture the illusion of movement in still images.

camera film.) The rotating shutter cuts off the light at regular intervals, to break the action up into a series of images.

Projecting the movie

The projector at the cinema contains a lamp and a lens to direct light through the film and onto a screen.

With 24 frames being projected each second, a movie uses a lot of film. This is cut into lengths called reels. Cinemas use two projectors. As soon as one completes its reel, the other starts up.

▼ A thaumatrope is a cardboard disc with an image on each side. If you spin the disc, the two images merge to make a single picture. The thaumatrope shows how your eye can be fooled by fast-moving pictures.

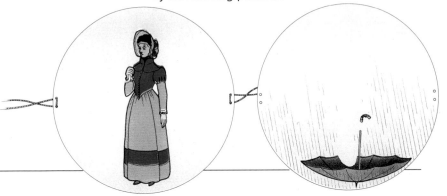

TIME-LAPSE PHOTOGRAPHY
A movie camera takes 24 frames every second. If you take one frame every hour, but project the film back at the normal speed, you can see a day's worth of frames every second! This means you can film something changing extremely slowly, such as a flower unfurling.

Cinema shows 24 frames a second, but TV shows 25. So, when you watch 25 minutes' worth of movie on television, you see it slightly fast – in only 24 minutes.

 key words
- camera
- frame
- projector
- reel

▼ The 1933 movie *King Kong* had some of the best special effects of its time. King Kong himself was a model, and in this scene he is set against a 'futuristic' background.

Sound
The movie soundtrack is on the same film as the pictures, sometimes as a patterned strip of light and dark down the edge. The projector shines light through this strip onto a light-sensitive circuit. This converts the pattern into an electrical signal, which is then turned into sound by an amplifier and loudspeaker.

Cartoons that move
Traditional-style cartoons and animations use models, puppets or lots of drawings, but modern animation is usually made using powerful computers. Feature-length cartoons can take years to produce.

As with an ordinary film, a series of images, each one slightly different from the one before, creates the illusion of movement. Puppeteers spend hours patiently moving the bodies of their puppets between each frame. Cartoonists create lots of drawings, each with a tiny change.

Traditional animation can be speeded up by using transparent plastic sheets called cells. The background artwork can remain the same while cells with drawings of the moving characters are placed on top.

BRINGING THINGS CLOSER

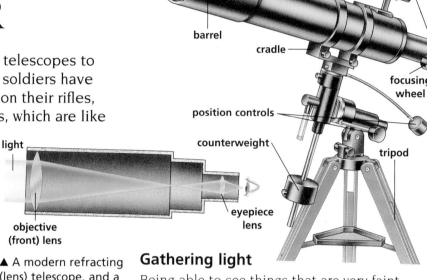

small 'finder' telescope
eyepiece
barrel
cradle
focusing wheel
position controls
counterweight
tripod
eyepiece lens

Astronomers use telescopes to study the stars, soldiers have small versions mounted on their rifles, and birdwatchers use binoculars, which are like a double telescope.

Telescopes do two jobs. They make things that are far away seem nearer (they magnify them) and they help us to look at things that are too dim to see just with our eyes.

light
objective (front) lens

▲ A modern refracting (lens) telescope, and a cutaway view showing how it magnifies a distant image.

Refracting telescopes

Lens telescopes are called refracting telescopes because they use a lens to refract (bend) light. A Dutch spectacle-maker called Hans Lippershey probably made the first telescope in 1608. We can imagine that one day he held two lenses up, looked through both of them – and was surprised at what he saw!

Word of Lippershey's discovery soon reached the great Italian scientist Galileo Galilei. In 1609 he made an improved telescope. It had a convex (outward-curving) lens at the front and a concave (inward-curving) eyepiece lens.

The big lens at the front of the telescope is called the objective lens. It gathers as much light as possible and produces an image inside the tube of the telescope. The second, smaller lens (the eyepiece) acts like a magnifying glass, producing a bigger version of the image.

Wrong way up

Unfortunately the final image through Galileo's telescope was upside-down. Modern telescopes for use on Earth have a different lens system, so that the final image is the right way up. A similar system is used for binoculars. However, using this lens system blurs the image very slightly. Astronomers looking at very small, dim objects prefer to have a clearer image, even if it is upside-down.

Gathering light

Being able to see things that are very faint is more important to astronomers than magnification, because even a magnified star still looks like a dot. For this reason, astronomical lens telescopes have to have very big objective lenses. The bigger their lens, the more light they can collect.

The problem with this is that large glass lenses are very heavy. The lens has to be held round the edge, otherwise the support

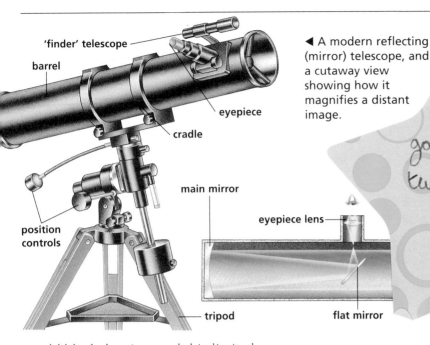

'finder' telescope

barrel

eyepiece

cradle

position controls

main mirror

eyepiece lens

tripod

flat mirror

◀ A modern reflecting (mirror) telescope, and a cutaway view showing how it magnifies a distant image.

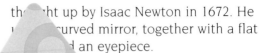

The antenna galaxy is actually two galaxys coliding together

...ght up by Isaac Newton in 1672. He ...curved mirror, together with a flat ...d an eyepiece.

...onian reflector, the concave ...thers the light and brings it ... There, a small ... the side of the ... by an eyepiece. ...ntages when it ...rst, as the mirror's ...the front, it can be ...ack. This is easier ...lens by its edge, so ...bigger. One of the ...rror telescopes is at Mount Paloma... ...fornia. Its mirror is 5 metres across – five times bigger than the largest lens telescope.

would block the view, and this limits how big a lens telescope can be (the biggest has a lens about 100 centimetres across). To see even fainter objects, a bigger surface to gather the light is needed. Since a lens will not do, a curved mirror is used to gather the light instead.

Reflecting telescopes

One of the most common ways of making a reflecting telescope, or reflector, was first

▶ The Antenna galaxy is actually two galaxies colliding together. An image from the Hubble Space Telescope (right) shows in incredible detail new stars being made in the central area. The best ground-based image (left) does not compare.

key words

- concave
- convex
- lens
- reflector
- refractor

◀ The highly advanced WIYN telescope is one of several telescopes on Kitt Peak mountain in Arizona, USA. A computer controls the shape of the main mirror and its surface temperature, to ensure the sharpest possible pictures.

The second advantage is that a mirror reflects all the colours of light in the same way. A lens will not bend all colours by the same amount, so the image in a lens telescope always suffers from some blurring of colours.

Top telescopes

The Keck I Telescope in Hawaii has a huge main mirror 10 metres across. It is made up of 36 hexagonal pieces 2 metres across. The images from a nearby second telescope (Keck II) are combined with those from Keck I to make an even better image. But ground telescopes will always produce slightly blurred images because of Earth's atmosphere. Being in orbit gives space telescopes such as Hubble a great advantage.

IT'S A SMALL WORLD

Imagine being the first person to look at bacteria and tiny insects through a microscope. You would have seen creatures to rival the scariest horror-movie monsters!

An ordinary (light) microscope makes very small things appear larger than life. It uses two lenses fixed at either end of a metal tube. The lens at the far end (the objective lens) collects light from the object and focuses it to make an image inside the tube. You look through the other lens (the eyepiece), which acts like a magnifying glass to enlarge the image made by the objective. Together, these two lenses can magnify the object by as much as 2000 times.

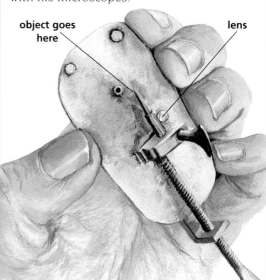
▼ A compound (many-lensed) microscope.

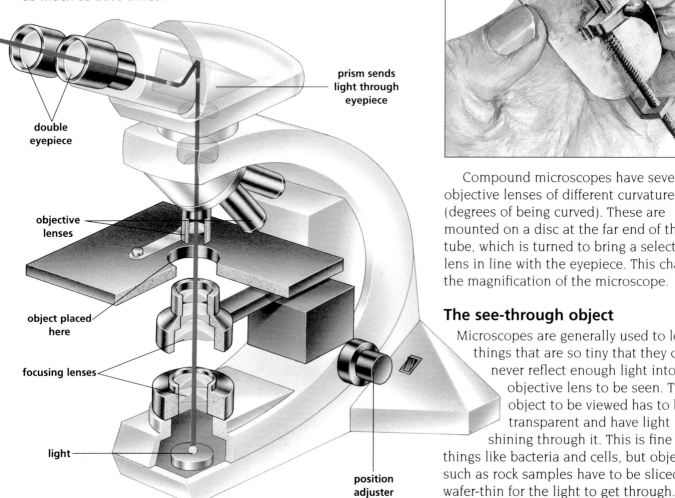

object goes here

lens

prism sends light through eyepiece

double eyepiece

objective lenses

object placed here

focusing lenses

light

position adjuster

Compound microscopes have several objective lenses of different curvature (degrees of being curved). These are mounted on a disc at the far end of the tube, which is turned to bring a selected lens in line with the eyepiece. This changes the magnification of the microscope.

The see-through object

Microscopes are generally used to look at things that are so tiny that they could never reflect enough light into the objective lens to be seen. The object to be viewed has to be transparent and have light shining through it. This is fine for things like bacteria and cells, but objects such as rock samples have to be sliced wafer-thin for the light to get through.

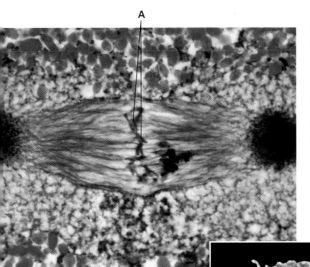

A

◄ ▼ Three photographs showing a cell's genetic material.

(a) A photograph of a dividing cell, magnified about 200 times. The genetic material is in the chromosomes (A).

The object is placed on a strip of glass (the slide) and positioned so that light passes through it. If the object is in a liquid, a tiny puddle is trapped between the slide and a small glass square (the cover slip).

Simple microscopes may have a mirror that is tilted to direct light onto the object, but larger ones usually have built-in lamps. They might also have a camera instead of an eyepiece, so that the object can be photographed.

The limits of light

There is a limit on how much a microscope that uses light can magnify an object, and how small an object can be seen through it. This is because light travels as a wave. Have you ever noticed that water waves will bend round rocks if the rocks are small enough? The same thing can happen with light. If the object is very tiny, the light waves bend round it, so it cannot be seen. To achieve really high magnifications and see minute objects, you have to use an electron microscope.

Electron microscopes

Electrons are tiny particles of matter that come from atoms. They have an electrical charge, so magnets can be used to change

the way they move. An electron microscope uses a beam of electrons instead of light, and uses magnets to focus the electron beams instead of the lenses used in a light microscope.

Some electron microscopes send electrons through a transparent object. These are called transmission electron microscopes. Others (scanning electron microscopes) bounce electrons off the object's surface while sweeping the beam back and forth. A computer examines how electrons bounce off the surface and build up a detailed picture. Electron microscopes can magnify objects by up to a million times.

(b) Electron micrograph of a single chromosome pair, magnified over 10,000 times. These are X and Y chromosomes (sex chromosomes). Females have two X chromosomes; males have an X (top) and a Y chromosome, as shown here.

(c) A scanning tunnelling microscope image of a section of DNA, the material chromosomes are made from. The image is magnified over 1½ million times. DNA has a double-helix (spiral) structure. The row of orange/yellow peaks in the centre are the individual turns of the helix.

🔵 key words

- electron microscope
- eyepiece
- light microscope
- objective lens
- scanning tunnelling microscope

State of the art

Scanning tunnelling microscopes (STMs) are the newest kind of microscope. An STM has a tiny, ultra-fine probe that is moved across the surface of an object. Electrons from the atoms on this surface jump onto the probe tip as it passes. By counting these electrons, it is possible to make an image of the surface capable of showing individual atoms.

LIGHTING OUR LIVES

The Sun is a huge nuclear furnace that constantly pours out light and heat energy. Without this energy the Earth would freeze and living things would die. But modern life does not stop when the Sun goes down. We have lights in our homes, headlamps on our cars and torches to carry around.

Burning materials such as coal or wood produce a fairly poor light, and once they are burnt, they cannot be used again. Electricity works much better. It tends to heat up any material it passes through. Once the material gets hot enough, it gets rid of excess energy by producing light.

The simplest electric lights contain a coil of thin wire called a filament. It is made of tungsten, a metal with a very high melting point. The filament is placed in a glass bulb filled with a small amount of gas – either argon or nitrogen. The gas stops the filament catching fire.

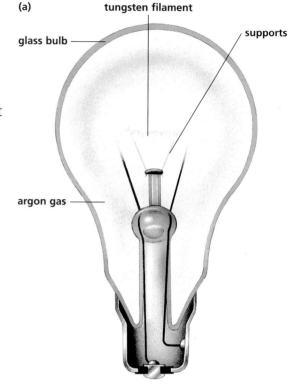

(a) tungsten filament

glass bulb

supports

argon gas

electrode   glass tube   phosphor coating

(b)   mercury vapour

▲ An incandescent (ordinary) light bulb (a) has a filament made of tungsten. An electric current heats the filament to about 3000 °C, making it glow. Electrodes at either end of a fluorescent tube (b) produce a current through the small amount of gas in the tube. The gas gives off UV light, which makes the phosphor coating glow brightly.

The filament glows brightly when a current passes through it. Over time, the filament gets gradually thinner until eventually it snaps. Then the light bulb must be replaced.

Special bulbs

Quartz-halogen bulbs are used in overhead projectors and spotlights. They produce more light and use less power than ordinary bulbs because they work at a

◄ Glow-worms make their own light from chemical reactions. Scientists are studying them – and using the chemicals they produce – to make new light sources.

much higher temperature. The type of gas used in these bulbs (usually iodine or bromine vapour) gives the filament a longer life. The bulbs are made from quartz rather than glass to survive the high temperature.

A fluorescent light is a glass tube containing a small amount of mercury vapour. When an electric current passes through the gas, it produces ultraviolet (UV) light. As we cannot see UV light, the inside of the tube is coated with phosphor, a material that glows when UV light hits it. It is this glow that we see. A fluorescent tube produces four times the light of an ordinary light bulb of the same power.

Discharge lamps contain a gas that produces visible light when you pass a

key words

- bulb
- filament
- fluorescent light
- laser
- LED

▼ The bright lights of the big city. In Las Vegas, USA, the many casinos and hotels compete for attention with brilliant neon signs.

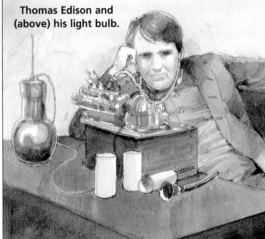

FATHER OF LIGHT
Thomas Edison (1847–1931) was one of the greatest inventors that ever lived. In 1879 he demonstrated his electric light bulb to the public. It worked by passing an electric current through a thin filament made of carbon, which then glowed brightly. Other inventors also made light bulbs, but Edison went further. In 1885 he opened a power station that supplied electricity to power his bulbs.

Thomas Edison and (above) his light bulb.

current through it. Sodium street lamps use a thin vapour of sodium and glow a bright yellow colour. The many different coloured lamps used to make advertising signs are made the same way. They use the gas neon, mixed with other gases chosen to make different colours.

LEDs and lasers
Light-emitting diodes (LEDs) are small electronic lamps. They come in different colours and are used in hi-fis and radios to show when the power has been turned on. Infrared LEDs are used in TV remote controls. Some modern LEDs are bright enough to be used for car brake lights.

Lasers produce very concentrated light – usually in a tiny beam that is less than a millimetre across. This makes lasers unsuitable for lighting a room, but ideal for some very special uses – such as reading data off compact discs, welding things together or carrying out delicate surgery.

THE LIGHT FANTASTIC

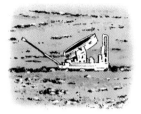

On the Moon is a mirror the size of a tea tray. It was left there by the first astronauts on the Moon. This tiny target is used to reflect back a laser beam sent from Earth – a distance of nearly 400,000 kilometres!

Lasers are useful for all sorts of jobs, because they are so controllable. Doctors direct their heat to weld (fix) retinas in place at the back of the eye, reshape the cornea and seal leaking blood vessels.

Lasers are also used to drop bombs with great accuracy – a laser-guided missile can demolish a target leaving neighbouring buildings untouched.

Surveyors and builders sometimes need to line things up very accurately – for example, if they want to measure heights or mark where a wall should be. A laser is the ideal tool for this, too.

key words

- atom
- coherent light
- hologram
- laser

◄ Lasers have a variety of uses in eye surgery, including re-attaching the retina (the layer of light-sensitive cells inside the eye) if it comes loose. Patients do not need an anaesthetic for this treatment.

Straight lines

Lasers are a special source of light called coherent light. This means that all the light waves they produce are in step with each other and travel in the same direction. This is different from a light bulb, which produces light travelling in all directions.

▼ The ruby laser was the first laser invented, in 1960. A high-intensity light produces a bright flash to start the laser. Atoms of chromium within a rod of artificial ruby are excited by this light flash, and emit red light.

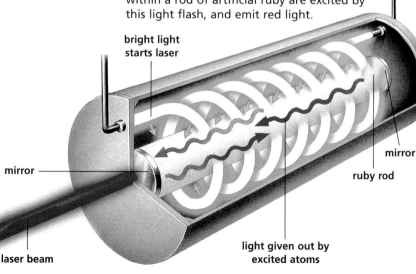

bright light starts laser

mirror

mirror

ruby rod

laser beam

light given out by excited atoms

◄ This green laser beam is used to create an artificial 'star' high in the atmosphere. Astronomers can measure changes in the shape of this 'star' caused by the atmosphere, then use this information to improve their images of real stars.

Another difference is that a light bulb will seem dimmer if you stand a long way from it. This is because the light spreads out – the further away you are, the less light enters your eye. Laser light hardly spreads out at all. It can be sent a very long way – to the Moon and back – without becoming much dimmer.

Heat and colour

Concentrated light from the Sun can set fire to a piece of paper. A powerful laser can do the same, because all the energy in the light is concentrated into one small spot. Very powerful lasers can even cut through metal. Laser cutters guided by computers are used by manufacturers to carve pieces of metal very precisely into complicated shapes.

Light is a kind of wave. The white light from a light bulb is a mixture of light of many different colours, each of which is a different wavelength. Laser light, however, is a single, pure colour. Each type of laser produces light of one particular wavelength.

'Laser' stands for 'light amplification by stimulated emission of radiation.' In other words, a light source is made stronger (amplified) by rays (radiation) that are given off (emitted) by atoms that have been given extra energy (stimulated).

How lasers work

A laser works by making an atom produce light, and forcing the atom next to it to make the same light. It's rather like having a row of dominoes standing up – if you knock one over, the rest fall in sequence.

Lasers have either a crystal inside them or a tube containing a gas or liquid. There is a mirror at either end. Electricity (or a flash of bright light) is used to give energy to the atoms in the laser material. They get rid of this energy by sending out light waves. This triggers other atoms to send out the same waves. The light builds up inside the crystal and reflects from a mirror back down the crystal again, triggering more atoms as it goes. The light carries on again, back and forth, getting steadily stronger. One of the mirrors is not perfectly reflecting, and the laser beam eventually escapes at this end of the tube.

THE MAGIC OF HOLOGRAMS

In 1947, the British physicist Dennis Gabor (1900–1979) worked out how it would be possible to record a three-dimensional image on photographic film. No one was able to try out his ideas until the 1960s, when the laser was invented. The first hologram was made in 1962, but a laser had to be shone through the film to make the picture visible. Advances since then have made it possible to make holograms that can be seen in normal light. Holographic images are used on credit cards to make them less easy to copy.

BOUNCING BEAMS

The journey starts at the touch of a button. Into the tunnel they dive, bouncing one way then the other. They crash against the walls, but keep moving at the fastest possible speed. A hundred kilometres later, the light waves emerge from the tiny glass wire.

Optical fibres are thin strands made from glass or plastic. They are usually about one-eighth of a millimetre in diameter. These amazing fibres play a vital role in science, medicine and communications.

Fibre optics in medicine

Doctors use endoscopes, which have optical fibres to carry light into the body and bring a picture back. They can be used to see inside a person's stomach to find ulcers and other problems. It is not very comfortable having a tube pushed down your throat, but better than being cut open.

For keyhole surgery (operations performed through a small hole), surgeons use endoscopes fitted with little tools. A small hole is cut in the skin and the endoscope is pushed in. The optical fibres allow the surgeons to see what they are doing.

Getting the message

Optical fibres are also used in communications. They carry TV and radio signals, telephone messages and other information. A device sends the information as pulses of infrared light. Fibres can carry far more information than electrical wires.

▶ The inner and outer cores of an optical fibre are designed so that nearly all of the light bounces back when it tries to escape. The light can travel up to 100 km without getting much dimmer.

cladding

core

light bounces off surface of core

key words

- endoscope
- keyhole surgery
- optical fibre
- reflection

◀ A single optical cable contains hundreds of optical fibres. These fibres are conducting white light.

MAKING COPIES

Long ago, the only way to make copies of books was to write them out by hand. This was a job that monks were specialists in. Their work was beautiful – but took years to do. With modern photocopiers we can make hundreds of copies in minutes.

A photocopier 'reads' a piece of paper that you put onto it and prints a new copy. It uses light to read the paper, and static electricity and ink to make the copy. The process is called xerography, a word meaning 'dry writing'.

To use a photocopier, you place a page upside-down on a glass screen. The photocopier moves a light across the page from beneath. The light is reflected off the white parts of the page, but not off the black parts (the writing or image). A lens directs the reflected light onto a flexible belt, which has already been given a positive electric charge. Where light falls on the plate, the charge leaks away.

key words
- photocopier
- toner
- xerography

There is now a 'copy' of the image on the belt, written in electrical charge.

Toning up

A black powder called toner is sprinkled onto the belt. The toner has a negative electric charge. It sticks to the positively charged parts of the belt, but does not stick to the rest.

Next, a piece of paper is pressed against the belt, on top of the toner. Another electric charge transfers the toner onto the paper. At this stage, the toner is on the paper in the pattern of the original writing, but it is not fixed. It can easily be smudged or blown away.

Finally the paper is warmed by heated rollers. This melts the toner particles, forming a sticky ink which quickly dries on the paper. The copy is now ready to be pushed out of the machine.

▼ A modern photocopier is a complex device. Light from the page being copied is projected onto a belt (or drum) charged with electricity. Where the page was light, it causes the electrical charge to leak away. The dark areas of the page keep their charge, and black toner powder sticks to these areas. The toner is transferred to a sheet of paper, then fixed by heat.

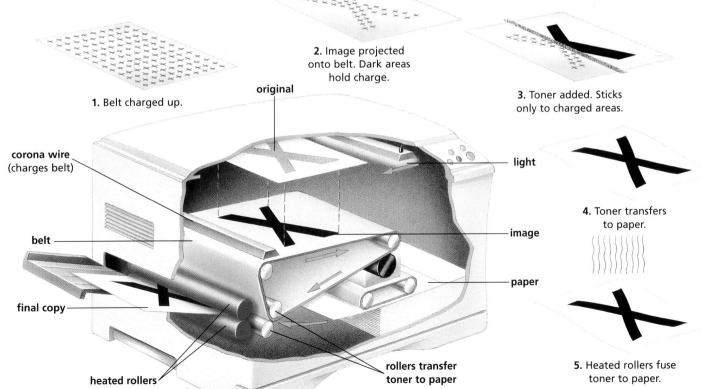

1. Belt charged up.

2. Image projected onto belt. Dark areas hold charge.

3. Toner added. Sticks only to charged areas.

original

corona wire (charges belt)

light

belt

image

final copy

paper

heated rollers

rollers transfer toner to paper

4. Toner transfers to paper.

5. Heated rollers fuse toner to paper.

VISIBLE AND INVISIBLE WAVES

Imagine it's a sunny day and you're listening to the radio. The ultraviolet rays from the Sun are giving you a tan, and you are very warm, so you are giving off infrared rays. Radio waves, ultraviolet and infrared rays are just some of the invisible waves that belong to the electromagnetic spectrum (range).

Colours are part of this spectrum, too. Since we can see them, we say they are part of the visible spectrum. Blue and red are at opposite ends of the visible spectrum.

Waves of light

Light travels as a series of very tiny waves, rather like ripples spreading out over a lake. The waves are tiny electrical and magnetic disturbances. That is why they are sometimes called electromagnetic waves.

All waves have their own wavelength and frequency. The wavelength is the

▶ A photograph of a shower taken by a camera which detects infrared (heat) radiation. The different temperatures are shown in the picture as different colours, ranging from red (hot) to blue (cold).

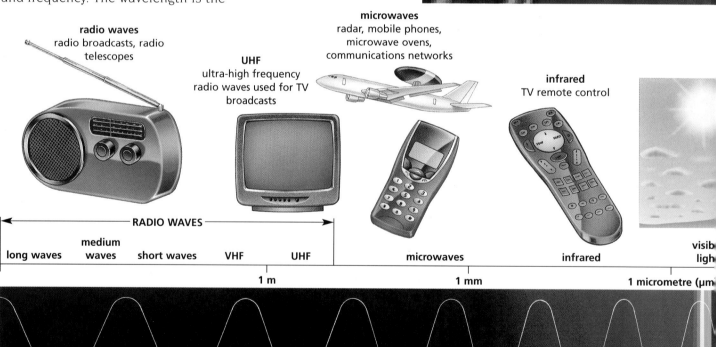

radio waves
radio broadcasts, radio telescopes

UHF
ultra-high frequency radio waves used for TV broadcasts

microwaves
radar, mobile phones, microwave ovens, communications networks

infrared
TV remote control

RADIO WAVES

| long waves | medium waves | short waves | VHF | UHF | microwaves | infrared | visible light |

1 m   1 mm   1 micrometre (μm

wavelength

LONGER WAVES, LOWER ENERGY

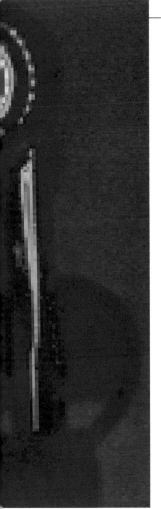

distance between peaks on the wave – for visible light, this is very small. The frequency is how many times the wave vibrates (shakes) each second.

'White' light is really a mixture of all the colours in the rainbow. Each colour has its own wavelength, blue having the shortest wavelength and red the longest. But light is only a small part of the full range of electromagnetic waves. There are similar, invisible waves, some with wavelengths much longer than red light, others with shorter wavelengths than blue light. The complete range is known as the electromagnetic spectrum. Like light, all these kinds of wave can travel through the vacuum of space, and they move at the speed of light (300,000 km/s).

Radio waves

There are radio waves everywhere. We use them to send messages to each other and to broadcast music and television programmes. This is possible because we have found a way to alter radio waves, so that their pattern carries all the information needed for radios, TVs and telephones to recreate sounds and pictures. Each programme or channel has a specific frequency that the radio or TV can tune to.

Radio waves also come from the Sun and outer space. Astronomers use special radio receivers (called radio telescopes) to listen to them. The radio signals tell them about fantastic things going on in deep space, such as fast-spinning pulsars and dying galaxies.

Not just for cooking

Microwaves are a broad band of electromagnetic waves with a shorter wavelength than radio waves. Mobile phones use microwaves to send words and information to a receiver. Recently, people have become quite worried about this. It is possible that the waves from these phones are harmful to the brain.

Radar uses microwaves, too. A radar aerial sends out pulses of microwaves in all directions and then sweeps round to pick up any reflections coming back. Ships use radar to detect other craft at sea.

Microwave ovens use microwaves to heat food. The wavelength is carefully chosen so that it is easily absorbed by water molecules. The energy transferred in this way warms the water up. Most food has a lot of water in it, so this is an effective way to cook it.

Heat waves

Anything that is warm produces infrared (IR) waves – including you. The hotter a thing is, the more IR it produces. Night-vision goggles and cameras work by detecting the IR given out by people and animals and displaying it as visible light.

Some electronic components (parts) in machines produce IR. These are used in TV remote controls to beam IR signals to the television. Many computers have IR transmitters and receivers which they use to send information to other computers.

X-rays
medical X-rays, baggage checking, X-ray telescopes

gamma rays
given off by radioactive materials, cosmic rays from space

visible light, ultraviolet (UV)
both from Sun, but most UV blocked by atmosphere

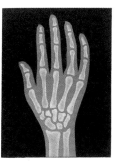

ltraviolet   X-rays   gamma rays

0.001 µm   0.00001 µm

SHORTER WAVES, HIGHER ENERGY

◄ The full electromagnetic spectrum. All the waves in this spectrum travel at the same speed – the speed of light. They all carry energy, but the amount of energy increases as the wavelength gets shorter.

Waves we can see

Visible light includes a very small range of wavelengths compared to the whole spectrum, but it is important because it is the only range of waves that we can see. When white light passes through a prism (a triangular piece of glass), the different colours in it are bent by different amounts because they have different wavelengths.

Burning waves

Ultraviolet (UV) waves can be harmful. Too much exposure to them can cause sunburn, blindness and skin cancer. The Sun produces a lot of UV. This would wipe out life on Earth if it all reached the planet's surface. Fortunately, we are protected by a layer of gas in the atmosphere (ozone), which absorbs most of the UV. Scientists are becoming concerned that some of the gases that industry produces are removing ozone from the atmosphere. As this could be very dangerous, people are working to cut down on the emission of these gases.

Some ultraviolet still gets through, so it is important to protect yourself in bright sunlight or at high altitudes, where the atmosphere is thin. Sun creams and sunglasses help to block UV. We all need some exposure to ultraviolet, though. Without it, our bodies would not be able to make vitamin D, which is important for keeping us healthy.

Amazing rays

X-rays have a shorter wavelength and more energy than ultraviolet rays. They have many uses. Doctors and dentists use

key words

- gamma ray
- infrared
- microwaves
- radiation
- radio waves
- spectrum
- ultraviolet
- X-ray

▲ A research scientist working on the Gammasphere, a sensitive instrument for detecting gamma radiation. The Gammasphere has been used to study collisions between the centres (nuclei) of certain heavy atoms, which briefly join to form a very large nucleus and then break up, releasing gamma radiation.

X-rays to make shadow pictures of the body so they can see broken bones or damaged teeth.

At airports, X-rays are used to check passengers' luggage. The X-rays pass straight through clothes but are stopped by metal objects, such as guns. X-rays also allow manufacturers to see inside a product, such as a television, and check that it has been put together correctly – without taking the whole machine apart.

JAMES CLERK MAXWELL

The Scot James Clerk Maxwell (1831–1879) was one of the greatest physicists that has ever lived. He made huge contributions to many areas of physics, but he will be most remembered for his work on the theory of electromagnetism. This built on the ideas of earlier pioneers such as Michael Faraday and led to the idea that light was an electromagnetic wave. Later, the German Heinrich Hertz used Maxwell's theory in his discovery of radio waves.

Danger rays

Gamma rays come from radioactive materials. They can be very harmful and they can pass through nearly all materials quite easily.

Gamma rays are used to kill cancers, but they have to be carefully controlled to prevent damage to healthy tissues.

Satellites have detected bursts of gamma rays striking the Earth from outer space. No one knows what causes them, but they are too weak to harm us.

AN INSIDE LOOK

X-rays

electron beam

vacuum tube

metal target

electrode

A priceless work of art is placed in an X-ray machine, while anxious dealers look on. Without damaging the precious surface paint at all, the machine might reveal previous sketches by the artist – or even a forgery!

X-rays are similar to light waves, but have a much shorter wavelength and a lot more energy. This makes them useful, as they can pass through most materials. It also makes them dangerous, as they can damage living tissues.

X-rays in medicine

X-rays will pass through most materials, but some X-rays are stopped by bones, which is why they are useful in medicine. Bones cast shadows when X-rays are shone on them. A photographic film can be exposed by X-rays that pass straight through the body. However, it will not be exposed in the bone's shadow. The developed picture clearly shows where the bones are. This is very helpful for doctors, especially if they want to see if a patient has broken any bones.

X-rays pass through soft body parts such as the stomach and intestines. Doctors can

▲ An X-ray machine fires a beam of tiny particles called electrons at a piece of metal. When the electrons crash into the metal, X-rays are given off.

look at these parts by feeding the patient a 'barium meal' – a mix of barium sulphate and water that absorbs X-rays.

A modern type of X-ray machine is the CAT scanner. This uses a computer to build a detailed picture of the patient's body by passing weak X-ray beams through it from lots of different directions.

The problem with using X-rays is that they can damage the body. There are strict rules about how many shadow pictures can be taken of a patient each year and the people who operate X-ray machines every day stand behind lead screens for protection while the picture is being made.

X-rays of high enough energy can also be used to kill cancers. This must be done carefully so no other parts of the body are damaged. One way is to use three weak beams that meet at the cancer to deliver enough energy.

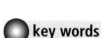

key words
- CAT scanner
- energy
- X-ray telescope

Space rays

The ability to see through things has all sorts of uses. In astronomy, for example, satellites carrying X-ray telescopes are mapping the Milky Way and looking for the strong X-ray sources that may be caused by black holes.

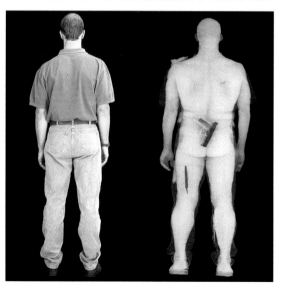

◄ An X-ray detector can discover hidden weapons. The X-rays pass through clothes and the body but are stopped by dense materials like metals.

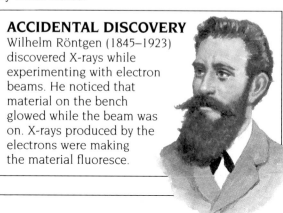

ACCIDENTAL DISCOVERY
Wilhelm Röntgen (1845–1923) discovered X-rays while experimenting with electron beams. He noticed that material on the bench glowed while the beam was on. X-rays produced by the electrons were making the material fluoresce.

VIBRATIONS IN THE AIR

Hummingbirds hover by flapping their wings very quickly, and their wings shake up the air as they move. The result is a beautiful humming sound.

When someone strums a guitar, you hear a sound. Strumming makes the strings on the guitar vibrate (shake) very quickly. The air carries these vibrations into your ear. Inside the ear, the vibrations are turned into electrical signals that are sent to your brain.

If you twang a ruler, it will wobble up and down. As it does this, it shakes the air particles around it. The shaking particles then make the air particles next to it vibrate as well – the vibrations pass from one set of particles to the next. All of these vibrations are sound waves.

▶ The loudness of a sound is measured in decibels (dB). This scale shows approximate decibel levels for familiar sounds.

▼ The violent vibrations of this pneumatic drill produce very loud sounds. Workers wear ear defenders to protect their hearing.

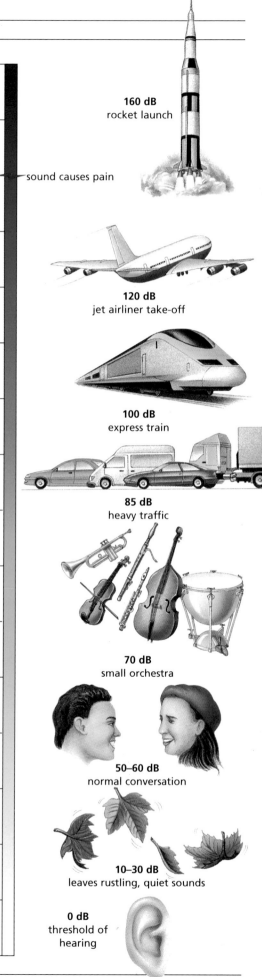

160 dB
rocket launch

sound causes pain

120 dB
jet airliner take-off

100 dB
express train

85 dB
heavy traffic

70 dB
small orchestra

50–60 dB
normal conversation

10–30 dB
leaves rustling, quiet sounds

0 dB
threshold of hearing

Humans make sounds with their voices. To do this, we blow air from the lungs past some tightly stretched cords in the throat (the vocal cords). These cords vibrate and set the air vibrating as well. To be useful, the vibrations must be made louder (amplified). Fortunately, the vibrations make the chest, mouth and throat vibrate as well. All these vibrations together make a sound loud enough to be heard.

High and low, soft and loud

A whistle makes a very high-pitched sound. The vibrations are very fast. A bass guitar makes a very low-pitched sound. Its vibrations are rather slow compared to those made by the whistle.

Every sound has a frequency. This is the number of vibrations made in a second. High-pitched sounds have a high frequency. Low-pitched sounds have a low one.

Humans can hear a range of different frequencies. The lowest sound we can hear has 20 vibrations in a second. The highest sound has 20,000 vibrations in a second. As you get older, you become less sensitive to high-pitched sounds. Some animals, such

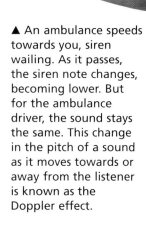

▲ An ambulance speeds towards you, siren wailing. As it passes, the siren note changes, becoming lower. But for the ambulance driver, the sound stays the same. This change in the pitch of a sound as it moves towards or away from the listener is known as the Doppler effect.

as bats, can hear much higher-pitched sounds than we can.

Some sounds are very loud, for example when a big truck rumbles past. Other sounds are very soft, such as the rustling of a field mouse. Loud sounds are made by big vibrations. Small vibrations make soft sounds. Listening to very loud sounds for a long time can damage your hearing. For instance, regularly listening to loud music through headphones can be bad for your ears.

Fast and faster

Sound waves travel through the air very quickly – 330 metres per second, or more than 1000 kilometres per hour. At that speed, you could travel the length of three football pitches every second.

Standing at a railway station, you can often tell when a train is coming because the tracks start to buzz. A little time later, you hear the train itself. This is because vibrations made by the train travel through the tracks as well as through the air and the sound travels more quickly through the tracks than through air.

Sound can travel through many different materials, which is why you can sometimes hear your neighbours through the walls! The denser the material, the more quickly sound can travel through it. Submarines

BREAKING THE SOUND BARRIER

The airliner *Concorde* and many military aircraft can travel faster than the speed of sound: they are 'supersonic'. The jet-powered car *Thrust* SSC travelled at supersonic speeds on land. The scientific term for the speed of sound is Mach 1. The fastest aircraft can fly at Mach 3 – about 3000 kilometres per hour.

People on the ground hear a 'sonic boom' when a supersonic aircraft flies over. This is caused by the aircraft squashing up air in front of it, creating a 'shock wave' that makes a loud sound.

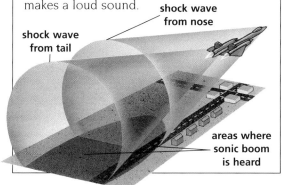

shock wave from nose

shock wave from tail

areas where sonic boom is heard

🔵 key words

- amplify
- decibel
- echo
- frequency
- Mach
- pitch
- supersonic
- vibration

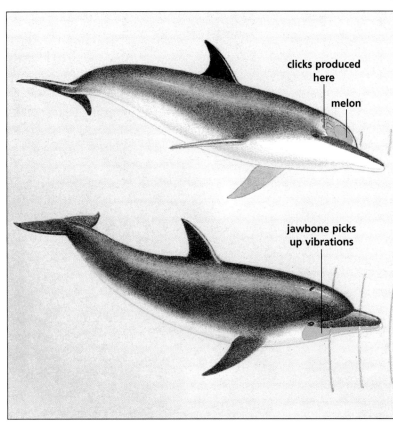

clicks produced here

melon

jawbone picks up vibrations

ANIMAL SONAR

Animals such as bats and dolphins can use short pulses of high-pitched sound to find their way around and hunt food.

Dolphins have a sonar system called echolocation. They make clicking sounds in air passages in their nose, which are focused into a 'beam' by an oil-filled organ in the head called the melon.

When the clicks hit an object, they bounce back as echoes. The dolphin picks up the echoes as vibrations in its jaw. The time between the echo and the click tells the dolphin how far away the object is.

By making a continuous stream of clicks and receiving echoes, the dolphin can get information about everything around it. It is like 'seeing' with sound.

sound 'beam'

sound bounces back from fish

use sound waves in water to detect ships. Water is denser than air, and sound travels five times faster through it. Sound can travel 15 times faster in steel than in air.

Echoes

If you make a loud noise in a large, empty room, you sometimes hear the noise repeated a few times. These repeated noises are echoes. Echoes are made when sound waves bounce off things. The echo arrives back a moment after the original sound.

When a sound wave hits an object, some of it will bounce off or be reflected. But some of the vibrations will be swallowed up (absorbed) by the object.

Soft objects tend to absorb sound, while hard objects reflect sound. That's why a room with no furniture is ideal for making echoes. The hard walls and floor reflect sound, and there are no soft sofas or carpets to absorb it.

▶ An echo-free chamber. The floor, ceiling and walls are made of glass-fibre wedges designed to absorb noise, so that no sounds are reflected.

SENSING VIBRATIONS

Hearing is very important in the natural world. Many animals have a highly developed sense of hearing. It is often easier to hear something that is trying to eat you than to see it – especially if it is hiding from you!

The ear is the organ we use to detect sounds. Sounds are made when objects shake (vibrate). These vibrations shake up the air to make sound waves.

Any organ that senses sounds needs three things. It has to have a way of collecting sound waves. It needs a way of making them stronger (amplifying them). And it needs to turn the amplified waves into electrical signals. Somehow, the brain turns these signals into the rich world of sound that we hear.

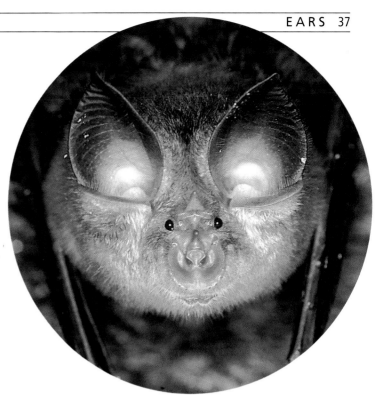

▲ A bat's ears are a vital part of its echolocation system. The bat compares the tiny differences between the echoes reaching each ear to help build up a picture of its environment.

The human ear

In humans the outer ear is funnel-shaped to help collect sound waves. The waves then strike a thin membrane called the eardrum, making it vibrate.

The other side of the eardrum is linked to a set of tiny bones (ossicles). As the drum vibrates back and forth, it pushes and pulls on these bones. Working together, the ossicles make the vibrations stronger. This is the amplifying part of the ear.

The bones strike a tiny membrane (the oval window), making it vibrate. On the other side of the oval window is the inner ear. This snail-shaped container (cochlea) is filled with liquid. The vibrations of the oval window make the liquid move about. Tiny hairs line the inner ear and wave about in this sloshing liquid. The hairs are rooted in sensitive cells. Triggered by the waving hairs, these cells send electrical signals to the brain.

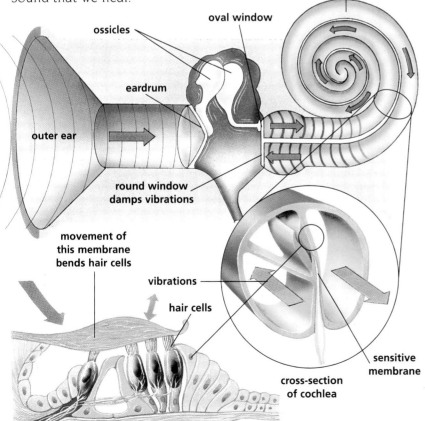

cochlea

ossicles

oval window

eardrum

outer ear

round window damps vibrations

movement of this membrane bends hair cells

vibrations

hair cells

cross-section of cochlea

sensitive membrane

nerves

◀ How the ear works. Sounds cause the eardrum to vibrate; the ossicles amplify these vibrations and pass them to the cochlea. Movement of the liquid inside the cochlea affects tiny hair cells, which send nerve signals to the brain.

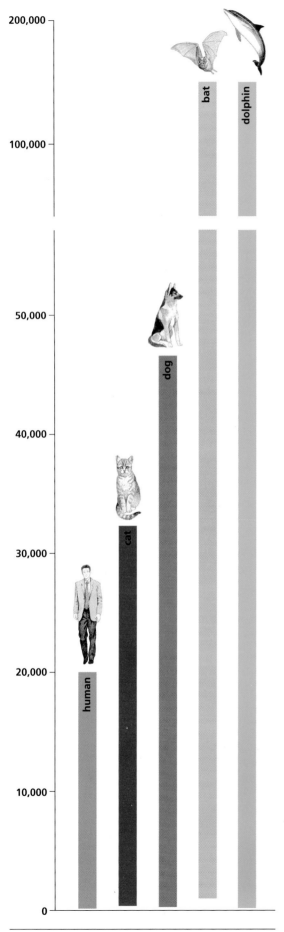

The chart shows sound frequency ranges (vibrations per second) for human, cat, dog, bat, and dolphin, with a scale from 0 to 200,000.

◄ Humans can hear deep hums as low as 20 vibrations in a second. The highest sound we can hear is about 20,000 vibrations a second – a kind of high-pitched hiss.

key words

- amplify
- brain
- eardrum
- ossicles
- sound
- vibration

Another part of the inner ear, called the semicircular canals, is not involved in hearing but is important for balance.

Other ears

All mammals have ears. Some of them, such as rabbits and the fennec fox, have huge ears in relation to their size. Large ears are very sensitive as they collect a lot of sound waves. Big-eared animals can often pick up sounds that are too quiet for humans to hear.

Bats are mammals that rely a great deal on their sense of hearing. Most bats live in the dark, so sight is not much use to them. They 'see' using an echolocation system. They make bursts of short, high-pitched sounds (too high for humans to hear), then listen for any echoes coming back. The pattern of echoes tells them about their surroundings. They can also track things they like to eat by bouncing sound waves off them.

Many insects that live on land hear with a small membrane on their legs. Spiders sense vibrations through their legs, often transmitted through the large webs that they weave. Fish have a 'sixth sense' – they have an organ (called the lateral line) down each side that can detect waves and gives them a form of hearing.

▼ Constantly being exposed to loud noises can damage your hearing. In the 1930s industrial workers like these did not wear ear protection, and many of them developed hearing problems.

HARMONIOUS SOUNDS

People have been making music since the dawn of time, and it has evolved into an incredibly varied collection of styles. One 20th-century composer wrote a symphony for full orchestra, accompanied by a washing machine and vacuum cleaner!

Music is a collection of noises that have been arranged to sound interesting. It can make you happy, sad, relaxed or excited. Some people enjoy singing or playing musical instruments. Others just like to listen to recordings or live musicians.

Sounds are made by objects that are shaking back and forth (vibrating). These vibrations can be very quick, or rather slow. Fast vibrations make sounds that have a high pitch. Slow vibrations make low-pitched sounds.

Each vibration has a certain frequency. This is the number of vibrations that occur every

▶ A singer with the flamenco group Los Activos. The human voice is the simplest musical instrument. The air in the throat is set vibrating by tiny strings called vocal cords.

🔵 key words

- frequency
- harmony
- note
- octave
- pitch
- scale
- vibration

second. The frequencies of sounds that go well together form a pattern. A sound of one frequency always goes very well with a sound of twice that frequency. Patterns like this make music.

Musical notes

Musical sounds are organized into notes. The pitch of every note is a certain frequency. A scale is a sequence of notes. Most scales used in Western music start with a note of one frequency and end with the note of twice that frequency. These two notes are an octave (eight notes) apart.

Harmony is created when two or more notes with different pitches are sounded together. The length of a note can vary too. The mix of long and short sounds adds rhythm, which is a very important element in all music.

Musical instruments

All musical instruments make vibrations. They are designed so the vibrations produce musical notes. There are three main types of instrument. String instruments make notes from vibrating

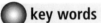

◀ Each key on a piano plays a different note. Several notes played at the same time produce a chord.

strings. Wind instruments have to be blown in some way. Percussion instruments have to be struck by something.

Sounds different

A guitar and a violin sound very different, even if they are playing the same note.

When an instrument makes a note, lots of different vibrations are produced. One of these vibrations will make the pitch of the note. It will be the loudest. Any other vibrations will be much quieter. The sound that we hear is made up of all these vibrations.

A violin will make one collection of vibrations. A guitar will make a slightly different collection. This is why they sound different.

▶ Electronic instruments make electric wave patterns similar to the sound waves produced by other instruments. These are then turned into sounds by loudspeakers. They can also take recorded samples of real sounds and change them in many different ways.

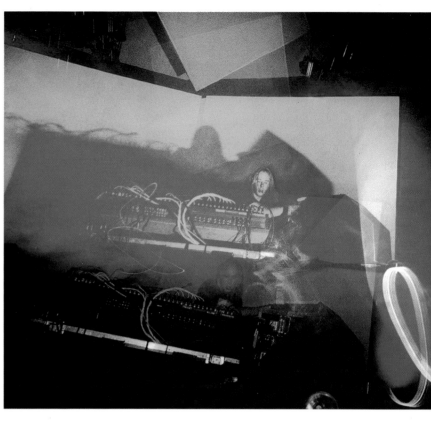

◀ How different kinds of musical instruments produce their sound.

sound waves

lips vibrate

mouthpiece

Brass instruments, like the trumpet, have an open mouthpiece. The trumpeter sets the air in the mouthpiece vibrating by 'blowing raspberries' into it.

vibrating reed

The saxophone, like the trumpet, is a **wind instrument**. The mouthpiece has a flexible reed, which vibrates to make sounds when the player blows it.

Guitars are **string instruments**. When a string is plucked, it vibrates to make a note. The guitarist can change a string's note by pressing the string against the guitar neck, which alters the string's length.

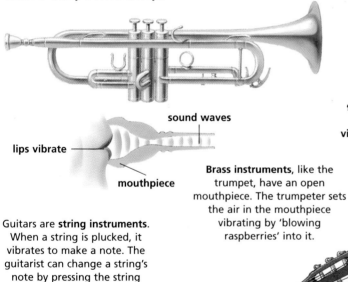

string vibrates

skin vibrates when hit

Drums are **percussion instruments**. Hitting the skin with a hand or a stick sets up vibrations in the skin, which makes a sound.

STORED SOUNDS

One of the strangest recordings ever made is winging its way through space. A long way from Earth, two *Voyager* space probes are heading for the stars. They carry recordings of sounds from Earth. Perhaps some day one of them will be found by aliens, who will play it back to hear what our planet is like.

Sounds are made by things that shake (vibrate). These vibrations shake up the air, making a sound wave. If the vibrations stop, the sound dies away. To record a sound, the vibrations have to be caught and changed into something else.

Sounds can be recorded using a microphone. This changes the sound vibrations into an electrical copy of the sound called a signal.

▶ This mini hi-fi system can play sounds recorded on cassette, CD or minidisc.

There are many ways of storing signals for a long time. One way is to turn them into patterns of magnetism.

In a recording studio, microphones are used to turn sound waves into electrical signals. These signals are made stronger (amplified) by special electronic circuits. The signals travel down wires to the mixing desk. Electronic instruments make their own electrical signals, which can be sent straight to the desk.

At the mixing desk, a technician controls the signals and mixes them together. Then they are recorded on to a large magnetic tape (the master tape). Copies can be made from the master tape in many different formats, including CD (compact disc), cassette and minidisc. Eventually, music will be sold on computer chips.

Replaying music

Once the music is stored in some form, it can be played back whenever you want. The player reads the stored music and turns it back into a pattern of electricity. This is then made stronger by an amplifier. From the amplifier, the electrical signals are passed to a set of loudspeakers. These turn the signals into vibrations of the loudspeaker cones, which we hear as sounds.

◀ In a modern recording studio, each instrument or voice is recorded separately on its own 'track'. The recording engineer uses a mixing desk to combine the tracks. He can control how loud each track is. He can also add echo or other effects.

▼ In a stereo recording, the sound is recorded as two slightly different 'tracks'. For example, an instrument may be slightly louder on the left-hand track than on the right. This will make the instrument sound as if it is closer to the left-hand loudspeaker.

Analogue and digital

The music on the master tape is recorded as a smoothly changing pattern – an analogue recording. The recording on a cassette tape is analogue too.

Analogue recordings are very fragile. They cannot be copied very often or they lose quality. These days most recordings are made digitally.

The first step in making a digital recording is to turn the music into a pattern of numbers (digits). This is called

▼ A microphone turns sounds into an analogue (smoothly changing) signal. In a cassette, this signal is copied directly onto tape. In a CD, the signal is digitized and the numbers are recorded as a pattern of bumps.

magnetic copy

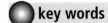

cassette

loudspeaker

analogue signal

analogue signal

microphone

signal recorded as pattern of bumps

CD

analogue signal

digital signal

10110010

● **key words**
- amplifier
- analogue
- digital
- master tape
- stereo

'Hi-fi' is short for 'high fidelity'. Fidelity means faithfulness, and so the name refers to systems that reproduce sounds that are faithful to the original recording.

sampling and is done by an electronic circuit. From here, the music can be stored in a variety of ways. On a CD the numbers are stored as a pattern of bumps. On a minidisc, they are stored as spots of magnetism.

The quality of digital recordings is very high. Once the music is in the form of numbers, it can be copied many times without losing any quality.

Stereo

A stereo recording tries to create the illusion that you are listening to real musicians in the room. It does this by tricking your ears. For stereo to work there must be two loudspeakers with some distance between them.

ELECTRICAL SOUND

Be careful what you say! Spies use special microphones to hear conversations from a long way away. The same microphones can also record birdsong from a distance. Later, the tape can be played back through a loudspeaker.

Microphones turn sounds into a pattern of electricity (an electric signal). Loudspeakers do the opposite: they turn electric signals into sounds that you can hear.

The need to shake

Sound is made by something shaking (vibrating). These vibrations shake up the air to make a sound wave.

Microphones have a moving part that can be shaken by a sound wave. Often this is a thin disc called a diaphragm. Different types of microphone use different methods for turning the vibrations of the diaphragm into electric signals.

In loudspeakers, electric signals produce vibrations in something that can shake up the air. Most loudspeakers

▶ The shell-shaped Nautilus speaker is designed to give outstanding sound quality, adding nothing and taking nothing away from the pure sound. It stands more than a metre high, and weighs 110 kg.

▶ How a condenser microphone works. Two thin plates carry an electric charge across them, which varies depending on how far apart the plates are. Sound causes one plate to vibrate. This change the distance between the two plates, causing similar changes in the charge on the plates.

cone

coil

magnet

▲ How a loudspeaker works. The loudspeaker coil is attached to the cone. An electric signal passing through the coil causes it to be attracted to or repelled from the magnet. This pushes and pulls the cone, making sound waves.

have cones that vibrate. A telephone's speaker uses a metal diaphragm rather than a cone.

Using microphones and loudspeakers

Microphones and speakers have many uses. Hearing aids use small microphones to collect sound. The sounds are then amplified and played back through a loudspeaker in the earpiece. Microphones and speakers are used for music concerts, and there is a loudspeaker in every TV. Telephones and most computers have built-in microphones and speakers.

fixed plate

moving plate (diaphragm)

🔘 key words

- cone
- diaphragm
- electric signal
- loudspeaker
- microphone
- vibration

MUSIC AND MORE

The ancient library at Alexandria, in Egypt, contained 500,000 scrolls, filling many rooms. Nowadays we can put the same amount of information on a few hundred CDs, which would fit on a couple of library shelves.

Compact discs (CDs) can store a great deal of information. Often this information is music. A CD-ROM is a compact disc that stores text (words), pictures, sound, computer games or computer software. The 'ROM' stands for 'Read Only Memory'.

The information is held on the disc as a series of bumps on its shiny surface. The bumps follow a spiral track, starting near the middle of the disc and ending at the edge.

The disc is read by shining a laser beam onto it. As the beam sweeps over the bumps, it reflects as a series of flashes which are picked up by a light-sensitive circuit and turned into electrical signals.

Turning sound into bumps

Sound is vibrations in the air. When a CD is recorded, the sound is 'written down' as a series of numbers, each recording the size of the sound vibration at a particular moment. With complex music, the vibrations change quickly, so the sound has to be written down thousands of times per second. On the CD the sound values are coded as binary numbers – numbers written using only 1s and 0s. Each bump is a 1, no bump is a 0.

▲ An electron microscope photo of the surface of a CD. The bumps are just 5 millionths of a metre across and about twice as long. The whole spiral track is over 8 kilometres long!

Other types of disc

Digital videodiscs (DVDs) hold even more information than CDs. They use smaller bumps and have two reflective layers. Recordable CDs (CD-Rs) do not have bumps. They use patches of colour on the disc to change the reflected laser light.

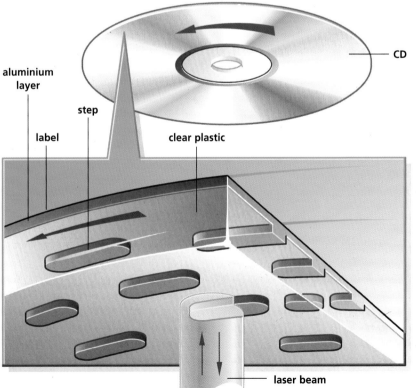

aluminium layer

step

label

clear plastic

CD

laser beam

◄ How a CD player works. The laser reads the spiral track by sweeping across the disc as it spins. A detector picks up the changes in the reflected beam when the laser hits a bump.

key words

- CD-R
- CD-ROM
- DVD
- laser
- spiral track

SECRET VIBRATIONS

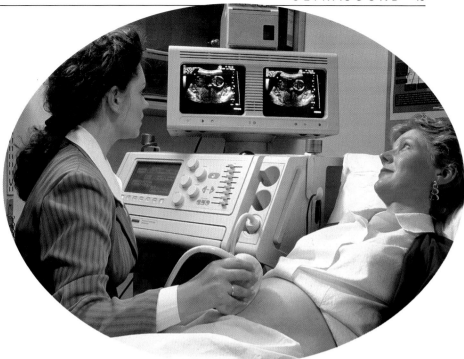

Blow a dog whistle and you might think that it was broken! The whistle's sound is so high-pitched that humans cannot hear it. Sounds that are too high-pitched for humans to hear are called ultrasound.

We cannot hear ultrasound, but we can make machines to produce ultrasound and detectors to measure it. Scientists have found many uses for ultra-high pitched sounds.

Using ultrasound in medicine

Sending waves of ultrasound into the body is a way of making a picture of what is inside. The ultrasound is reflected by organs in the body, and a detector collects the reflections. Computers can use the pattern these make to build up a picture. Pregnant women are often given ultrasound scans, so that doctors can see how their baby is growing.

Ultrasound can also be used to treat some medical problems. Sometimes tiny bits of solid matter can grow in the kidney.

key words
- hearing
- sound
- ultrasound
- welding

▼ An ultrasound scanner uses an electrical signal to make a special crystal vibrate fast enough to produce ultrasound waves. A detector in the scanner head picks up the reflected waves.

▲ Ultrasound scanners are used to check that a baby is growing well. You can see the baby moving about, and even watch its heart beating. Ultrasound is used instead of other types of scanner because it is very safe and will not harm the growing baby.

The result is a kidney stone. A beam of ultrasound can shake up kidney stones so much that they break up and can be passed harmlessly out of the body.

Melting metal

A very strong beam of ultrasound can even melt a piece of metal. Metal shapes can be cut out this way. Two pieces of metal can be joined together by melting them where they touch. They are then allowed to solidify. This is called ultrasonic welding.

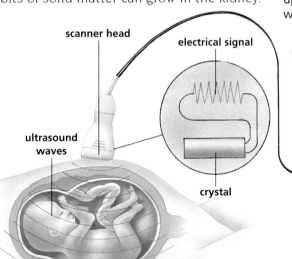

scanner head

electrical signal

computer turns pattern of reflections into a picture

ultrasound waves

crystal

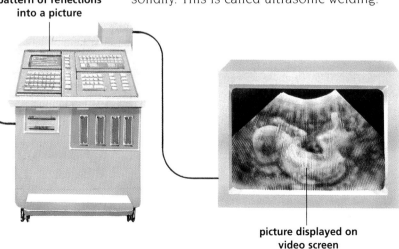

picture displayed on video screen

GLOSSARY

This glossary gives simple explanations of difficult or specialist words that readers might be unfamiliar with. Words in *italic* have their own glossary entry.

analogue Representing quantities or signals in a physical form. An analogue watch, for example, measures time by the position of hands on a dial. Compare *digital*.

camera A device that exposes *light* onto a film to record a picture.

colour A sensation produced by the eye and brain when *light* of a particular *wavelength* is detected. An object's colour depends on the wavelengths of light it produces or reflects.

compact disc A disc that stores information as a pattern of tiny bumps on a flat surface.

concave Of a *lens* or *mirror*, curved like the inside of a ball or circle.

convex Of a *lens* or *mirror*, curved like the outside of a ball or circle.

digital Representing quantities or signals by means of precise numbers. A computer is digital and represents data as a series of binary numbers, using 0s and 1s only. Compare *analogue*.

electromagnetic radiation A kind of *radiation*, including *light* and ranging between radio *waves*, which have long waves, and gamma *rays*, which have very short waves.

endoscope A medical instrument that uses *optical fibres* to see inside the body.

frequency The number of times a *wave* goes through a complete cycle of motion in a second. Known as the *pitch* in music.

hologram A three-dimensional image of an object made by storing the pattern of *light* it reflects.

laser (**L**ight **A**mplification by **S**timulated **E**mission of **R**adiation) A device that produces a thin, bright beam of *light* of a single *frequency*.

lens A curved piece of plastic or glass used to bend *light rays*.

light *Radiation* that stimulates the sense of sight and makes things visible.

light year The distance that *light* travels in one year (about 9.5 million million kilometres).

loudspeaker A device for converting patterns of electricity into sound *waves*. Often used to play back recorded music.

magnetic tape Material for storing sounds or pictures as patterns of magnetism. Cassette tapes and video tapes are examples.

microphone A device for converting sound *waves* into patterns of electricity. The electrical patterns can then be stored.

microscope An instrument that produces a magnified image of a small object.

mirror A shiny surface that reflects light and forms an image.

optical fibre A thin wire of plastic or glass along which *light* can travel very easily.

pitch The highness or lowness of a voice or musical note.

radiation Energy given off as *waves* or tiny particles. Heat, *light*, cosmic *rays*, ultraviolet light and sound are different types of radiation.

ray A thin line of *light*, heat or other *radiation*.

recording The process of turning sound or *light* into patterns of electricity that can then be stored.

reflection *Light* or sound bouncing back off an object.

refraction *Light* or sound *waves* changing direction as they pass from one material into an other.

retina The layer of light-sensitive cells at the back of the human eye.

spectrum The full range of *electromagnetic radiation*. Part of this range, the visible spectrum, can be seen by the human eye. Ultraviolet, X-rays and gamma *rays* are too short to be seen by the human eye. Infrared, microwaves and radio *waves* are too long to be seen.

telescope An instrument that produces a magnified image of a distant object.

ultrasound Sound *waves* of a *frequency* too high for humans to hear.

wave The way in which heat, *light*, sound or electricity travels.

wavelength The distance between two peaks on a *wave*.

X-ray A type of *wave* that can pass easily through materials that are not very dense. X-rays are often used to inspect the insides of objects, including the human body.

INDEX

Page numbers in **bold** mean that this is where you will find the most information on that subject. If both a heading and a page number are in bold, there is an article with that title. A page number in *italic* means that there is a picture of that subject. There may also be other information about the subject on the same page.

ACKNOWLEDGEMENTS

Key
t = top; c = centre; b = bottom; r = right; l = left; back = background; fore = foreground

Artwork
Baker, Julian: 6 tr; 8 c; 10 b; 42 t; 42 br. Birkett, Georgie: 25 tr. D'Achille, Gino: 5 tl; 32 bc. Franklin, Mark: 14 br; 17 bl; 22 bl; 20–21 tc; 30–31 b. Full Steam Ahead: 5 tr; 13 br. Hawken, Nick: 7 cr; 8 tl; 9 bl; 18 br. Jakeway, Rob: 8 tr; 9 br; 28 cl; 43 tr; 43 b. Morris, Tony: 25 tr. Oxford Illustrators: 18 tr. Parsley, Helen: 22 cr; 39 bl. Saunders, Michael: 12 b; 12–13 tc; 37 bl. Smith, Guy: 4 c; 11 b; 16 cl; 24 tr; 26 br; 29 b; 33 tr; 34 cl; 40 b; 45 b. Sneddon, James: 44 bl. Visscher, Peter: 4 tl; 7 tl; 10 tl; 13 tl; 16 tl; 20 tl; 22 tl; 24 tl; 26 tl; 28 tl; 29 tl; 30 tl; 33 tl; 34 tl; 39 tl; 41 tl; 43 tl; 44 tl; 45 tl. Wood, Michael: 38 cl; 36 t; 37 tl.

Photos

The publishers would like to thank the following for permission to use their photographs.

B&W Loudspeakers Ltd.: 43 c.
Canon: 11tr; 14 tl.
Corbis: 5 cr (Charles & Josette Lenars); 7 tr (Galen Rowell); 15 c (Ales Fevzer); 34 bl (David Reed).
Digital Vision: 38 br.
Kobal: 19 br (RKO).
NASA: 21 cr (Brad Whitmore (STScI)).
Oxford Scientific Films: 8 bl (John Downer); 14–15 tc (Raj Kamal); 19 cl; 24 bl (Jorge Sierra); 37 tr (Carols Sanchez); 45 bc (Colin Monteath).
Photodisc: 6 br.
Redferns: 40 tr (Jon Super); 39 tr (Henrietta Butler).

Science and Society Picture Library: 17 tc, 18 c (National Museum of Photography, Film & TV).
Science Photo Library: 4 tr (Martin Bond); 7 bl (Royal Observatory, Edinburgh); 10–11 tc (NASA); 14 b (William Ervin); 13 bl (Guy Felix/Jacana); 13 bc (Eye of Science); 20–21 bc (David Parker); 23 tl (CNRI); 23 c (Biophoto Associate); 23 cr (Lawrence Berkeley Laboratory); 25 bl (Alex Bartel); 26 bl (Will & Deni McIntyre); 26–27 tc (David Parker); 27 br (Colin Cuthbert); 28 bl (Adam Hart-Davis); 30–31 tc (Dr Arthur Tucker); 32 tr (Lawrence Berkeley Laboratory); 33 bl (American Science & Engineering); 35 tr (Rafael Macia); 36 br (Crown copyright/Health & Safety Laboratory); 41 bl (C. S. Langlois, Publiphoto Diffusion); 44 cr (Dr Jeremy Burgess); 45 tr (Saturn Stills).
Sony: 9 br.
Sony UK Ltd.: 41 cr.